MY CHILDHOOD
— IN —
NAZI GERMANY

Elsbeth Emmerich
with
Robert Hull

Editor: Catherine Ellis
Designer: Nick Cannan

First published in 1991 by
Wayland (Publishers) Ltd
61 Western Road, Hove,
East Sussex BN3 1JD

© Copyright 1991 Wayland (Publishers) Ltd

British Library Cataloguing in Publication Data
Emmerich, Elsbeth
  My childhood in Nazi Germany.
  1. Germany. Social life, 1933-1945 – Biographies
  I. Title   II. Hull, Robert
  943.086092

Hardback ISBN 0 7502 0077 4
Paperback ISBN 0 7502 0286 6

Typeset, printed and bound
by Butler & Tanner Ltd, Frome and London

Picture Acknowledgements

The publishers would like to thank the following for allowing
their photographs to be used in this book: Mary Evans *back-ground to cover*; Imperial War Museum 16, 39, 45, 46, 60, 62, 73,
79, 85, 90; Peter Newark 23, 89; Popperfoto 37, 55, 69, 70, 82, 86,
95; Topham Picture Library 75, 77, 80; Wayland Picture Library
Title page, 18. The remaining photographs all belong to Elsbeth
Emmerich. The artwork on pages 35 and 41 was supplied by
Peter Bull.

CONTENTS

Introduction

This is the story of my childhood in Germany during the war of 1939 to 1945. It's about all the things that happened to me and my close family – my mother, my father, my two sisters, and my grandfather and grandmother. Grandad and grandma were my mum's father and mother and lived with us most of the time. They were my only grandparents. My dad's father and mother had already died.

Our family was really much bigger than the one round me, though. My father was very close to his family. He had a brother, Willy, and seven sisters: Elly, Hanni, Greti, Lotti, Fränzi, Erna and Maria. My mother had two sisters: Anni and Elfriede. Most of them married, so I had lots of aunts and uncles!

In my story you'll hear about Erna and Fränzi and a bit about Elly and Elfriede. But mainly you'll hear about my close family. What I've written is told partly from what I remember and partly from my dad's letters. He was called up into the army on 30 November 1939, and while he was away fighting he wrote letters to all of us: to my mum, to us children, to his brother and all his seven sisters.

Many of these letters from him were lost, but many survived. Aunty Fränzi kept hers, and she let me have them – along with Aunty Elly's – to help me write this book. Before Aunty Elly died, she let Aunty Fränzi have her letters. Aunty Maria still has hers. Quite recently my mother burnt all the ones my father had written to her. I would have loved to read them, but of course it was her right to destroy them if she wished.

Dad in France, 1940.

My dad was a keen photographer, and we have photographs from his time in the army, in France and Russia, as well as other family photographs, like those of dad's car, and the ones he took when we moved into our new house.

You might have guessed something important and sad about this story already. I don't think it's a sad story though. I'm not sad reading it, and I wasn't writing it. Our life during the war was awful in some ways, but looking back now I think more of how we helped each other, and how brave we had to be, and how we were even happy at times.

Margret, Elfi, mum and me, in Düsseldorf, 1940.

CHAPTER 1
The New House

Our new house was just outside Düsseldorf, and specially built so that our grand-parents could live with us. When we arrived it still wasn't finished. There were piles of sand and cement and builders' tools lying around, and we had to walk up wooden planks to the front door. We went inside and some workmen in the bathroom told my father that the copper wash-tub hadn't come, so mum wouldn't be able to do the laundry.

I remember what happened next that day because it was the first time I heard about 'the war'. First a man came on a bike and said that the copper tub wouldn't be coming at all. The Führer needed all the copper in Germany for the war. Then two

Myself, with a large paper-cone of goodies on my first day at school, Easter 1940.

more men came with a big flag-pole and a big flag – the swastika. They dug a hole in the muddy patch that was to be our garden and planted the flag-pole in it.

I was five.

One day, a few weeks after we had moved in to the new house, I found my father in the garden, working on a big piece of wood. I asked him what he was doing. 'Making a bed,' he said. We all had lovely beds. What did he need to build a bed for?

'Who for?' I asked.

'For mum,' he said, 'an extra one to go in the cellar.'

Mum wouldn't sleep in the cellar. He must be teasing.

A day or two later he was working at the front of the house. He was putting black paper over all our windows and the glass panels in the front door. I asked him why. 'No light must shine through,' he told me.

'Why not?' I asked.

'Because the enemy would see.'

I didn't understand that either. But I decided 'the enemy' must be something to do with 'the war' that they'd started talking about, so it was perhaps alright.

One day I realized it wasn't alright. I heard mum and dad talking in whispers in the kitchen. Mum was crying. Dad put his arm round me and told me not to cry as well. One of my uncles 'had fallen' in the war in Poland. If I'd fallen it wouldn't make anyone cry except me, so it must be something different, I thought. Something serious must be happening.

Next I heard my grandparents and mum and dad talk about 'the fighting'. There must be a quarrel going on somewhere. Gradually I got used to the idea of 'the war'. This war had all started when we moved into our new house.

Dad with his youngest sister, Aunty Maria.

Settling In

My parents had saved up all they could to buy this house. They had wanted one big enough for all of us: the two of them, Margret and me, and our grandparents. Now they were beginning to get settled. My father was only twenty-five, but he was already a master butcher and worked for himself at the abattoir.

Even though he was working so hard, dad always had time to spend with us. At the weekend there would be friends and relatives calling, or he would take us in the car to the River Eifel or the Mosel. There he would buy bottles of good Mosel wine to take home.

Both my parents liked cooking and they often used to have friends round. If I had to go to bed I sometimes crept downstairs and hid behind the sofa to listen. Then my parents would find me and send me upstairs. They were quite strict. Once my mum had said 'No' it stayed 'No'. Tantrums were no use. My dad would spoil us, and give us toys and pretty things, but he wouldn't stand any nonsense.

Myself at my grandparents' grave in Düsseldorf, in 1940.

Rose and Albert, who lived next-door-but-one, became special friends. They didn't have children yet, and would sometimes lean out of the window and watch us. Rose had been friendly with my mum from the time they'd worked at the Co-op. I thought she was very pretty, like Snow White, with her black hair and white skin. She seemed to like us, and sometimes would call us over and give us sweets. She told my mother how different my sister and I were, how I would close the door quietly behind me before I looked round and ventured out, whereas my sister was half-way down the path when the door slammed shut.

A great deal needed doing in the house. When my mother wasn't cooking and baking she was buying new things or making curtains. Soft beige was a fashionable colour at the time, and my mother soaked the Brussels lace in weak tea.

Outside, my father and grandfather were sorting out the wilderness, trying to turn a building site into a garden. They planted trees and shrubs, made paths and laid paving stones. They sowed a lawn in the front, and the back was dug over ready to grow vegetables. Gradually it all began to take shape.

They did all this garden-making and tidying as well as going out to work. My father used to get up and leave very early, so I did too. I wanted to get up when he did. After getting his breakfast my mother would go back to bed, but I'd often stay downstairs. One morning, to give me something to do and not disturb her (or Margret who was only two) she found me a shopping bag and asked me to pick up some wood for the fire.

My father used to deliver fish in his spare time.

I found some specially nice bits sticking out of the ground here and there, the right size for a fire and not dirty. They were just what I wanted. I collected them and took them inside to the kitchen.

It was quite cold that day so we had a fire. Half-way through the morning my mother came in and asked me where I'd got the wood from. I said I would take her outside and show her. Our neighbour was outside too, peering round here and there. He looked quite funny. Then mum told me what he was doing.

He was looking for the little wooden sticks he'd put in the ground to show where our garden ended and his began. I suddenly realized what I'd done. I'd felt very proud at the beginning of the day, but now I didn't. It was even worse later, because when their friends called, mum and dad would insist on telling them this really funny story of how Elsbeth collected the next-door neighbour's boundary stakes for firewood ...

Parents can be very embarrassing.

30 November 1939, the day dad left for war. From left to right, Aunty Elly, Dad, my cousin Karin, Uncle Victor, Aunty Maria, my cousin Heinz, Aunty Greti, Aunty Fränzi, my cousin Margret.

Off to the War

One day I saw a lot of my dad's things on my little table, neatly folded and stacked. There was even one of my toy cooking pots, filled with potato salad. When I asked mum what was going on she told me dad had to go away for a while. He had been 'conscripted'. That sounded official, but I still didn't understand. What was 'conscripted'? Why should my daddy be going away? Without me? Me, his favourite girl. Where was he going? When would he be coming back? And what about my little pot? Would I be getting that back?

I felt very put out. I looked over the items on my little table. There were neatly folded clothes, toilet articles, a packet of needles, reels of coloured cotton, shirt buttons and a pack of cards. There was dad's favourite food, *Frikadellen*, or fried meat balls, as well as a fried chop, and sandwiches wrapped in silver foil.

Mum didn't say much that day. Often when they were in the kitchen together I'd hear such screams of laughter from her, that I'd run in to see what was wrong, and she would just laugh and say, 'It's alright darling'. But today there was just silence.

Then I remember being woken up. Dad was leaning over me, saying goodbye. I hugged him so close, I didn't want to let go. He held me tight.

'Don't go, Daddy! Please don't go!' I cried.

'I have to,' said my dad in a broken voice. 'I'll be back soon. You be a good girl for mummy.'

Then he was gone. It had all happened so quickly. That was 30 November 1939.

I soon realized that the war was the reason for my dad going away. He was 'in

Margret and I.

the war'. It was strange to start getting letters and postcards from him, thinking he was a soldier in the army, and a long way from us. One of the first said: 'Dear all, have just received your parcel and was delighted with it. The chop was lovely.' He said army food was awful, so mum and her seven sisters sent little parcels of smoked sausage, pork chops, biscuits and cakes, and a cigar or two.

He also complained of pain in his feet. As a child he had caught polio, and always had stiffness in his toes. After sitting down, he had to get up slowly, getting his feet used to a standing position. In the army his pride hurt, because when he complained the other soldiers thought he was trying to get out of the war. At least that's what he thought, and it made him miserable.

But he talked most about home. He wrote about trying to get leave home and how difficult it was. He would say how dreadfully he missed all of us. He told us things about the army too. Once he wrote about going on an army exercise, when he had to lie in the snow for three-quarters of an hour. His clothes were frozen and stiff like a board.

I started writing to him too. I hadn't started school yet, but mum had begun to teach me how to read and write. This is a postcard I wrote to him when I was about five-and-a-half: 'Dear Daddy, We want a baby for Easter and we want you to come and see us. Lots of kisses, from your Elsbeth and Margret.' I knew I was going to have another brother or sister because mum had told me, after dad had gone.

Soon we heard that he was in hospital, having treatment for his feet. Travel was difficult, but mum was able to visit him at the hospital, and she stayed with him for

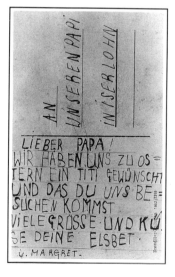

The postcard from me to dad, just before Elfi was born.

two-and-a-half days. It was a lovely time for them.

He had to stay in hospital for five weeks, and while he was there my sister Elfi was born, on 17 March 1940. She came before the midwife arrived. Grandad had gone off on his push-bike to fetch her, but before the midwife got to our house my grandma had already wrapped Elfi up. Elfi was very small, and she caught whooping cough, as did Margret and I. Visitors to the house thought Elfi wouldn't live. It was a terrible time for my mother.

But Elfi survived, and the next thing I knew was that dad suddenly came home! I can't remember feeling happier than when I held him tightly round his legs. I couldn't reach right round, because he was wearing all his soldier's outfit and seemed to be twice as big as usual. He also had a beard and I remember being slightly fussed about that. I never liked kissing him when he had stubble on his face. Margret, however, didn't mind his stubble, and she flung herself round his neck, leaving the legs for me to hug.

Dad sent us this postcard on 12 December 1939. The picture is of a war memorial to the soldiers who died in the First World War.

CHAPTER 2
Starting School

I was nearly six, old enough to start school. I was really looking forward to it. I loved reading fairy stories, and mum had taught me to write letters to dad. I had even made a little book of my own first poems, with my own drawings. It was a very small book, but I was very proud of it.

Mum took me to school the first morning. I liked it straight away! There was a big Easter bunny drawn in coloured chalks on the blackboard, and each of the coat hooks had a small picture on it, so you could easily remember which was yours. But I'd only just hung up my coat when mum came along with the teacher to say we'd gone to the wrong school.

Off we went to the right school, which sadly wasn't as nice. Our teacher, Frau Borsig, was a short fat lady who wore flowing dresses. She was very strict. One day when a boy in my class wanted to go to the toilet she told him he had to learn to manage like the others. It made us go completely quiet, then a few minutes later the boy stood up and started crying. He'd done it on the floor. Instead of feeling sorry for him Frau Borsig was cross and told another boy to take him home.

Things like that made us try to keep on the right side of her. One morning, I was on my way to school with two friends, Gisela and Albert, and we decided to pick flowers for Frau Borsig. There were buttercups and forget-me-nots in the field opposite the church. I felt like Little Red Riding Hood, straying off the path. We didn't notice the minutes passing and when

we got to the school everyone had already gone in. We could hear the class singing *'Deutschland, Deutschland über alles.'*

We pushed open the big door and peered in very anxiously. Frau Borsig, who was conducting, gave us a stern look and pointed towards the corner. We walked across in front of all the class and stood in the corner waiting for the singing to stop, our wet bunches of flowers dripping on the wooden floor.

At last there was silence, but when we tried to offer our flowers to Frau Borsig our gifts did not melt her heart a bit. Quite the opposite. First she was very cross and told us off for being late, then she snatched the flowers from our hands and threw them in the bin. It was awful. Everybody was staring at us. I was very hurt. No more flowers for this teacher, I thought to myself.

One thing she did like to receive from us was 'Heil Hitler!' Every day we had to greet her, and other grown-ups, with the

My school photo. I am on the far left in a white cardigan.

salute. I was used to doing this, but it still embarrassed me. On my way to school one day I went into a busy shop without making the greeting, thinking no one would notice. But a shop assistant pounced on me, saying angrily, 'Don't you know the German greeting?' She made me walk out and come back into the shop again, using the right greeting. I must have blushed to the roots of my long plaited hair as I held my arm out and said, 'Heil Hitler!' in a pretend grown-up voice. Then she started talking loudly to the other customers about children's bad manners nowadays.

The war followed us to school, with the sound of the air raid drill. When the siren went we had to line up in twos and march in silence to the air raid shelter. It had bare brick walls and no windows. We were made to sit back-to-back on wooden benches. There were first-aid boxes, and gas masks hanging on hooks on the wall. They frightened me. We had to practise putting the gas masks on, and then sit there in silence till the siren sounded for the end of the drill. We didn't even get the chance to make those lovely rude noises you could make inside gas masks. Then we would go back to the classroom, still in silence.

A group of JM (Young Girls) giving the Nazi salute. It used to make me really embarrassed to have to greet grown-ups with the salute, and the cry 'Heil Hitler'.

The drill used to upset me so much that when the siren went one day for a real alarm, I just ran off home. All I could think of was being with my mum and sisters and grandparents. An air raid warden shouted after me in the street, but I kept on running. I got home exhausted but safe.

Even though I didn't like my teacher, I liked reading and writing, and I did my work well. One day I was given a real postcard as a merit mark. I was learning to write the old German script, and sitting outside the house at my little table that evening after homework, I wrote to my dad, saying that Elfi was crawling already and would soon come for walks with us. I ended with lots of love and kisses and the sentence I put on every card: 'When are you coming to see us?'

I used to draw him pictures and decorate my letters to him. He would send me postcards with pictures of little girls who somehow looked like me, either because they had plaits, or wore dresses like mine, or were sitting down writing. I was always waiting for the postman to bring me his cards and letters. Once I had learned to read the old German script he would try his hardest to use that style of writing.

On my sixth birthday a big parcel arrived from my dad. In it was a coffee-set, very well wrapped up so nothing was broken, and two wind-up toys as well, for me and Margret. Mine was a Disney dwarf with a lantern and a pick which he could swing up and down. Margret's was a Donald Duck, who quacked and waved his arms about. I kept the coffee-set like a sacred possession. Not one piece was broken, until a few years later Margret dropped the coffee-pot. I couldn't forgive her, not for a long time. My dad had sent it.

Some of my drawings that I sent to dad. One of them shows a plane dropping bombs on soldiers below.

Letters from France

My dad was in France. The first letter from there was dated 4 June 1940. It said that he was stationed in a nice old castle, about 250 kilometres east of Paris. He hoped to be home soon, in September or October, because the war would be over by then, he reckoned. He was taking pictures of the war, and was now in charge of the kitchen. Mum said this would suit him, because he was a good cook, as well as having a large appetite – and cooks don't usually go short of food, even in wartime, she said!

One day he went to Paris and from there sent three pairs of shiny patent leather shoes for me, Margret and Elfi. Elfi's were tiny, and she hardly wore them because she was still in a push-chair, but Dad loved to spoil us – and mum. Once, when she was in a shoe shop and couldn't decide which

The German artillery riding through the streets of Paris in June 1940.

Dad (the one seated on the right) with some friends in a café in France.

pair of shoes she wanted, he told the salesgirl to wrap them both up. He would always arrange for big bouquets of flowers to be delivered on her birthday.

Then a more serious-sounding letter arrived. He said that something was going on that he couldn't write about. He asked my Aunty Elly to stand by the phone and he would tell her more. (We didn't have a phone at home. Phones were only for people who needed them for running their businesses. Two of my aunts had phones, and mum would go into town to receive calls from dad at their houses.) Perhaps the news was about being sent to the front, because these ominous words came at the end: 'I'm not afraid to be sent to the front, but I do think a lot about Grete and the children ... I am glad my mother is no longer alive because I would not like to have caused her all this worry.'

Dad and his fellow soldiers, drying out their clothes after getting soaking wet trying to repair a bridge. Dad is wearing his pullover on his legs!

There had been a very strong bond between my dad and his mother. He was the second boy among seven sisters and when he was struck down by polio my grandmother carried him every day to the banks of the Rhine to cover his limbs in the warm sand. She massaged him and looked after him and he recovered completely, except for the shortening and hardening of the sinews in his toes.

In his letters dad always talked about coming home, either on leave or at the end of the war. One day mother was at home making redcurrant jelly, with Aunty Fränzi and Aunty Elly along to help. We were talking about my dad, when grandad came home and said he'd been slowed down because there were a lot of soldiers being moved through the town. My aunties stayed on a bit longer, to avoid being delayed in the crowded streets. Eventually they left, Aunty Elly driving dad's old lorry, 'Gottfried', with Aunty Fränzi the passenger. But a minute or two later there was the wheezy thumping noise of Gottfried again. They'd come back, but this time, to our delight and amazement, with my dad!

What a noise and hubbub there was! It was all very hectic and happy, with the adults talking so excitedly we could hardly get a word in.

Dad told us about his journey on the way back from France. There were lots of French women and children on the train, and some children in his carriage were crying. My father offered them some of his chocolate and biscuits – the chocolate and biscuits he'd saved from his rations for us. By the time he arrived in Düsseldorf it was all gone. Not one single bar of chocolate left! He'd given it all away. Of course, when we got over our disappointment we were proud of him. One of the French women even wrote a little note thanking him for his kindness.

But the main thing was that he'd come home on leave. He'd arrived in such a surprising way, too.

Aunty Fränzi never tires of telling the story of how they'd seen a soldier thumbing a lift, and she suddenly found herself screaming out in sheer joy and excitement, 'Elly, it's Heinz!' It was 14 July 1940, and my dad's name-day. It was *Namenstag* for my mother the day before, 13 July. My Aunty Fränzi had always said, 'He'll be home on his name-day.'

Dad's old lorry, which we called Gottfried.

CHAPTER 3
A Birthday

Dad soon went back to the war and we did our best to make life pass as normally as possible. It was very difficult. We missed him too much.

One morning I was playing in the front garden, when along the road came a nicely dressed man and a little girl. She had a lovely pale lilac dress on, made of a fine voile, with a velvet band tied loosely round the waist. I gazed at her in admiration.

The man was looking at the houses as they walked along. As he passed ours he called out to me. 'Is your father here?' he asked me.

'He's away at the war,' I said.

'Is there anyone else at home?'

'Yes,' I replied, and told him who was in. He said he'd like to speak to my grandad, so I rang the doorbell for him.

Grandad came to the door and invited the man in, while I stood on the step with the girl in the lovely dress. I couldn't hear what they were saying inside, but soon they came out into the garden and grandad started to put up the flag-pole! Then he went indoors again, and emerged a minute later with the huge black and red flag with the swastika on it and hoisted it. He had an angry look on his face and seemed to be muttering. There was something going on he didn't like.

When the flag was up and the swastika was billowing in the breeze the man and the girl left. Watching them walk away down the road, looking at the houses, I suddenly felt suspicious of them. I guessed that somehow the 'nice' man had forced my grandad to do something he didn't want to.

I only found out later that it had been Hitler's birthday that day. Everyone was supposed to put out a flag, and when the man saw there was no flag flying in our garden, he stopped to make sure that we put one up. I had no idea at the time that no flags fluttered in my family's hearts for Herr Hitler. That was why no one had said it was his birthday.

A Nazi rally. The Nazi flag, the swastika, was a very important symbol. Every household was meant to have one.

Grandad

With my dad away I spent a lot of time with grandad. Sometimes I'd help him in the garden. He was a keen gardener and seemed to grow everything: lettuces, tomatoes, beans, onions, leeks, beetroot, parsley, radishes, herbs and lots more! He was always saying that children should get good fresh vegetables and fruit. He told us it was very important to eat things like spinach and carrots, fresh salads and berries. He'd make sure we ate our porridge in the morning, always mentioning how strong horses were and they were fed nothing but oats.

Meals were the same as before dad went away. We usually had a three-course meal, with soup – usually a clear soup with fine vegetables and noodles – then meat and vegetables, then pudding. We always ate at the dining-table, and put on a white table-cloth. It was lovely coming back from Sunday morning walks to find the table laid ready, and to the lovely smell of soup, the Sunday joint and the vegetables.

Most Sundays grandad would take us for a walk in the woods. Just below the wood he would stop at a kiosk to buy us a twisty sugar-candy stick or a lollipop. He loved the country in the same way as he loved his garden. He knew every bird by its call, and he could identify any feather we found on the ground. When he was young he had wanted to be a forest warden, but his parents could not afford to pay for the training he would need. Instead he became a blacksmith, and then later an engineer in a factory.

On one of these Sundays, when the world seemed to be perfect except for the absence

of my dad, there was a ring at the door.
Grandma answered it, and in came two
men in civilian clothing. I can't remember
what was said, though they wished us
Guten Appetit, and talked about the
weather while they waited for grandad to
finish his dinner. Then, while we were still
eating, grandad got up from the table.
Grandma helped him into his coat, and off
he went with these two men.

I didn't think anything more about it at
the time, except that perhaps it was
something important. Grandad was a
popular man. He helped people when they
had mechanical problems, and at the
factory where he worked he was always in
demand to repair machinery. So at the time

Me with grandad in
1940.

there was nothing unusual to me in the small scene I had just witnessed.

Much later, my mother told me the true story behind it all. It was the Gestapo who came that morning – to arrest grandad! He had been known to them since before the war for his anti-Nazi activities, and being a union shop-steward and a member of the Communist Party. There had been many visits to the house, though I hadn't really taken any notice of them. They had been watching him long before my parents married. When dad was eighteen he was beaten up by young fascist thugs because they knew he was dating my mum, and they didn't like grandad's anti-fascist views.

The Gestapo kept arresting my grandfather, but he was always released after a while. He was one of the best men in his engineering works, and desperately needed, and with some clever persuasion his boss managed to get him freed each time.

It would have been much too dangerous to let children in on the truth about these things at the time. We only learned about them after the war, so that many things became clear then which I had never really understood before. That was when I found out why there were times when I couldn't go with grandma when she took a cooked lunch to my grandad, in pots wrapped in tea-towels. I could go when she was taking it to the factory, but not when she was taking it to the prison.

They tortured my grandfather at the prison, trying to make him give them the names of those who were working against the Nazi regime. It didn't succeed. They took grandma, mum and two of her sisters to the prison and made them cry out for grandad to hear. That didn't work either.

A Summer and Winter of Waiting

Dad liked getting letters and postcards from me, and I used to like writing them to him. Some got lost, but this is one that survived. I wrote it in May 1940, about a month after my sixth birthday: 'Dear Daddy, I'll quickly send you a postcard. Do we have to wait long before you come on holiday? It is such a lovely summer. Many greetings and kisses, Your Elsbeth.'

For a while we didn't know where dad was. We had some letters from him marked *'Ort Unbekannt'*, meaning 'Origin not known'. In one letter dated 3 August 1940 he said how cold it was. He had moved camp, and while the men were loading the train there was a great downpour which soaked them. They didn't get a chance to change their clothing for two days and had to travel in unheated carriages, in a continuous shiver. He thought he would soon be moved to the front, perhaps to the east, but it might be to the Balkans or Africa, where the German troops had been quite successful. He said that by November he would have been a year in the army. He'd stopped smoking and drinking, and was spending all his free time in bed dreaming of home. Time went faster when you were asleep, he said.

But instead of being moved to the front he was moved to Thorn, 'the bug barracks' as he called it. It sounded awful: 'Socks and shoes are permanently damp and we've forgotten what it is to be warm. Heating hasn't been heard of. We shall probably stay here till 30 March and I don't look forward to the cold winter. I haven't had

Dad's letter to Aunty Elly from 3 August 1940, saying he had moved camp, and how cold it was.

any mail from any one at home, not even Grete. One feels totally lonely and lost out here, as if one had committed a big crime and been sent here to be punished.'

I remember addressing letters to Thorn, and posting them in a letter-box on the way to school. Paper was getting scarce, and we wrote on mauve letters with gummed edges, to save envelopes. He stayed there the whole of that winter, and was still there when he wrote to us a few months after Christmas.

This studio photograph of mum was taken in 1939. Dad used to carry it with him in his wallet when he was in the army.

And so we had our second Christmas
without him. It was very strange, feeling
all the excitement of Christmas but
knowing he was spending it somewhere
else far away. It made it seem less real,
somehow. But I do remember one moment,
standing with my sister outside the living-
room door on Christmas Eve, looking
through the frosted glass at all the colour
and light gleaming and shining through.
Mum was decorating the Christmas tree,
which in Germany is only put up on
Christmas Eve. We would see the tree and
all its magic as part of giving gifts early on
Christmas morning.

My mother liked an all-silver tree. There
were silver birds with long white tail-
feathers and silver bells and white candles,
and at the moment we entered the room
mum lit some sparklers. It was magical, like
something from the Snow Queen's palace!

I can't remember the presents I was
given, except for one, a beautiful china doll
with long dark plaits and a pink velvet
dress with a silk inset and collar. There
were tiny pearl buttons dotted down the
front. I loved her immediately and learnt
later that it was grandma's idea to buy it,
even though I already had two dolls, a soft
baby doll called Inge and a celluloid doll
with moveable limbs and blue eyes called
Ulli. For a long time I didn't know what to
call her, but her dark hair was like both
Aunty Maria's and Aunty Lotti's. Mum
said why don't you call her Marie-Lotte?
So I did and she became very special to me.

Soon the excitement of Christmas was
forgotten, and I went back to being at
school and wondering a lot about dad in
his cold barracks. He had been right
thinking he would stay there all winter. He
was still there when he wrote to us in April.

Margret and I in our
back garden in
Düsseldorf.

The card dad sent me for my seventh birthday.

Dad (on the left) as a machine-gunner.

He said he was now a machine-gunner. He was still waiting to be moved and couldn't stand the boredom. He said there was talk of trouble at the Russian border, where the German armies were losing men. He couldn't understand why his division, the 6th Panzer division, was still hanging about waiting for action. And as usual, he complained about the food, and asked for more film for his camera.

30 April 1941 was my seventh birthday. I was weeding the garden with my mother when the postman came. He spoke to me, 'I have something here for a birthday girl,' and he handed me a postcard. On the front was a little boy in a Hussar's uniform, touching his cap in greeting and holding in the other hand a bunch of roses. It was to me, and said, 'Dear Elsbeth, many happy returns on your 7th birthday from your daddy.' The card was written in the old German style I was learning at school and I could read it by myself. I felt very proud. But it was the second birthday my dad had been away.

CHAPTER 4
The Last Visit

Soon my mother received a letter posted in an ordinary post-box with a stamp. This happened sometimes when my dad wasn't allowed to use the army mail, or wasn't supposed to say where he was. This time the postmark was Königsberg, in East Prussia. It filled my mother with panic.

On 21 May 1941 he wrote to say that so many troops were going east he wondered if there was going to be a war with Russia. He said that he had asked for my mother to be allowed a visit, and been given permission. In no time she had packed some things in a suitcase and grandad was taking her to the station.

My mother stayed in Riesenburg, near Königsberg, with a family called Schmid. It had taken my dad two days of knocking on people's doors to arrange it. The Schmid family were very nice to my mother. I remember her saying how the children were so helpful to her, and did everything to make her stay comfortable. She talked particularly about Hermann, who was at the grammar school, and was then drafted into the SS, like all high school leavers. Afterwards my mother kept in touch with them by letter.

She arrived on the Saturday, feeling very well, but tired. She and my dad spent two lovely days together and each evening he had his meal with my mother at the Schmid's. My dad wrote to Aunty Fränzi near the end of mum's visit: 'Unfortunately, it will all have to come to an end, because Grete has to leave now. I cannot say what will be happening to us, and what I want

Frau Schmid, the woman my mum stayed with in Riesenburg.

to write I'm not allowed to write, but go to Grete next week and she will be able to tell you. We can forget about an end to the war, because it will probably go on for a long time yet.'

My dad.

My mother didn't even have the chance to say goodbye to him. When she went to the barracks the following morning, the troops had moved out in the night. My dad could not have known what was going to happen, or he would have said something to my mother. My mother arrived back home devastated, but glad she had seen him. It was the last time she saw him alive.

To Russia

My dad had been right, guessing that the troops going east were bound for Russia. After mum's visit we soon heard from him that he was in Russia, near Leningrad. Not much more than a month after she had seen him, he wrote to say that the night before he'd had the first mail from home for eight days, while he was looking forward to five pieces of dry bread and some coffee. They were 90 kilometres from Leningrad, he said, and he and some other men had been lying in woodland listening to the radio. My dad had pulled a seat from a shot-up vehicle and was listening to some music, which made him cry. He'd been thinking, 'if only there was a letter from home,' when someone called out 'Mail!', and there suddenly were three letters, from my mum and Aunty Fränzi, which he spent the night reading.

From that time my dad's letters were full of the fighting. In one he said that so many had been killed that if the wind was from a particular direction there was a terrible stench from dead bodies. He called it 'this terrible war,' and asked how the mood was back home 'because it's often quite bad in the front line.' He nearly got into a fight with another soldier who dad said was being gloomy. But, he said, 'we can't have a mutiny or all our sacrifices will have been in vain.'

In a letter to Aunty Elly of 7 August 1941, there was more about his life at the front. He said that they had been lying all day in a trench less than a metre deep. They were part of an attack, and were surrounded by Russians and fired on day and night by tanks and artillery. 'Our position couldn't

A photograph dad took of some Russian prisoners of war. Some of them are women.

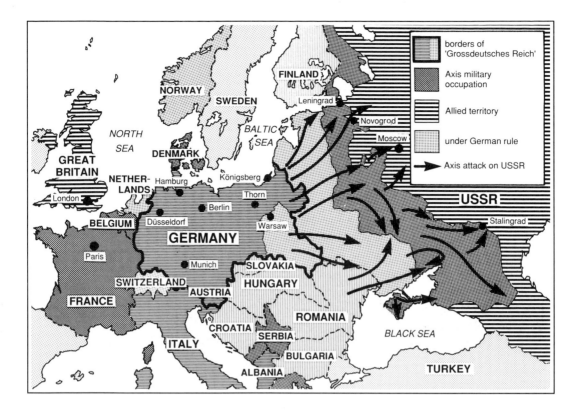

This map shows Europe during the war. You can see how far from home my dad was sent.

have been chosen better by the Devil himself. The worst things are all the snipers hidden in the trees. We are definitely sitting pretty.' The last three words were in thick ink.

In a solemn mood he went on: 'Do you think my Grete will marry again if anything should happen to me? Please bring me home if something should happen to me, because I would not want to stay here. Don't show Grete this letter. She doesn't need to read this, and anyway, I shall be returning home after this battle and we can all celebrate a wonderful victory together.'

I didn't read these letters till I was much older. It was hard enough then, at the age of seven, to cope with knowing that he was away fighting. It would have been much harder to bear if at the time I'd read some of his letters myself, right through.

War Reaches Us

While my father was in the thick of the fighting in Russia, we had been spared the worst of the war. We lived on the outskirts of Düsseldorf, in a part of the city which was of no particular importance to the enemy.

Then one night it all changed. We were in bed, and Elfi wanted to go on the potty. Grandma came in with a potty, and grandad, who'd also woken up, came in too. He told us to be quiet while he listened. He was by the hall window, listening to the noise of planes. Suddenly he yelled, 'Take cover!'

Mother sheltered Elfi with her body, and Margret and I pulled the eiderdown over our heads. There was the most frightening bang and roar and then it was quiet and we looked up. Grandma had been thrown against the wardrobe. The ceiling had come down and we could see the rafters. There was dust and a strange smell and a terrible mess everywhere. My mum grabbed us children. I don't know how she managed to take the three of us downstairs, when she was in bare feet and the stairs were strewn with rubble and broken glass. In the cellar we sat on the old sofa until the bed was made up.

Grandad went to examine the damage, with grandma. I asked her to bring my Marie-Lotte back down. I was petrified something might have happened to her. Mum said it wasn't the time to go looking for dolls, but grandma brought her down anyway.

In the cellar there were old newspapers and magazines. While we waited for grandad I remember looking at the

newspaper and seeing pictures of the
English royal family. It's strange that with
all the violence and horror going on above
I could still be intrigued by the two
princesses, Elizabeth and Margaret,
because they had the same names as my
sister and me.

Grandad came back and said there had
been a direct hit on our neighbour's house
and that he could hear people screaming
for help. He went off again, to see what he
could do, and returned a bit later with

Bomb-damaged
Düsseldorf. Düsseldorf
was badly damaged by
bombs. We had to leave
our home and move into
the country for safety.

another neighbour and between them the most frightening figure. It was a man in his long combination underwear. He was cut in so many places, I could not believe what I was seeing. His hair was matted with blood and dust.

We were moved from the bed back to the sofa. The man was laid gently on our bed and my mother and grandmother organized a bowl of water, clean towels and muslin. Carefully they dabbed at his face.

'Look, mummy, his eye,' I said quietly, pointing.

'His eye is running out,' my mother said to my grandmother.

The man was Rose and Albert's brother-in-law. His wife was also injured, but she was taken to another neighbour's cellar. An amazing thing happened to the old lady who lived at the top of their house. She had been thrown clean out of the house, in her bed, and landed in the street below, safely!

Then our door-bell rang. Two SA men came in. They had orders to get us out of our houses, because of unexploded bombs. We had to go to the local pub, where there were blankets and refreshments. On the way we met other neighbours. Werner, a boy of my age, came up to me.

'Rose and Albert are dead,' he said. 'Rose is decapitated and Albert's stomach is all out. My Daddy found them.' He sounded almost proud, giving this terrible news. I could not believe what he said. I started trembling and tears welled up. I didn't want to know any more.

It was a long walk to the pub. The night was now quiet, and the stars were out. At the pub there was that awful smell again, of explosives and mortar. Everyone looked dusty and messy. They were all talking, trying to be first with their stories. Mum

was quiet.

We didn't have to stay in the pub because we had relatives nearby, Aunt Klara and Uncle Willy, and we went to them for a few days. I liked being with my cousins. They were more adventurous than we were. My cousin Eleonore taught me how to use

A woman sitting outside her ruined house, weeping. The heavy Allied bombing raids meant that many people lost their homes.

eyebrow pencil. You burn a match down, and, hey presto, charcoal for the eyebrows. She used it on both of us and she taught me a new song: '*Im Grünewald, im Grünewald ist Holzaktion, ist Holzaktion, ahoi!*' It was a catchy number and she showed me a few dance steps. She went to ballet classes and knew about theatre things.

I was quite calm at Klara and Willy's, except whenever mum had to go off anywhere. I got upset then. I'd had a taste of war, and I was afraid of her leaving my side. Before I could let her go, she had to spend a lot of time reassuring me and promising that she'd soon be back safe and sound.

After a few days we were allowed back home, but only to pack our belongings. We were going away from the city, to the area of the country grandad came from. On our way we looked at the damaged houses. My friend Gisela showed me where her little brother had managed to crawl safely out of the rubble.

Coming back from her house, we heard a woman sobbing and lamenting. It was Rose's elder sister. She sat outside the bombed house and rocked backwards and forwards, throwing her head back each time. It sent shudders down my spine. I had never seen anyone in such distress. Years later, after the war, I saw the same kind of scene. I was in my back garden, and three or four children were playing in the field. Suddenly there was an explosion and screaming and I looked up to see the children thrown to the ground. An unexploded bomb had gone off. I passed the place a while later and saw the mother of one of the little girls who had been killed. She was rocking backwards and forwards the way Rose's sister had done.

CHAPTER 5
Escape to Altenkirchen

My mum told me we were going to stay with my Aunty Erna who lived in Altenkirchen with her parents, Uncle Gustav and Aunt Emma. Grandad and grandma had said they would stay and look after the house.

A map of Germany, showing the places we lived in during the war.

It was 17 August 1941 when we boarded the train for Altenkirchen, about 150 kilometres away. We children quite enjoyed the journey, except for waiting round on station platforms when we changed trains. When we arrived we went straight to their house in the High Street. They lived over Uncle Gustav's shop, which sold hardware and electrical goods. He also had a workshop down a little side road where he mended all sorts of things: pots and pans, lamps, milk-churns, anything.

We were welcomed with open arms and lots of sympathy. Aunty Erna was young and lively, with a mass of blonde curly hair which she usually wore up, with combs. My mother wore her hair in that style too, though she varied it and would sometimes just hold the sides back with combs and let it fall over her shoulders. In a different mood, she would wind it in a tight curl at the back.

I liked Erna a lot. She let us have her room to sleep in. It was to have been hers and her fiancé's when they were married, but Werner was reported missing at Leningrad and never came home. Over her bed was a picture of the two of them together. They looked a handsome couple.

Erna's parents were old-fashioned but very nice. Uncle Gustav was a thin man with a pair of small glasses on the end of his nose. He often listened to the radio, sitting right under the set mounted on the wall. They always listened for news about the Russian Front, and never quite gave up hope of Werner returning. Aunty Emma had a rounded figure, and wore loose-fitting clothes, with one apron on top of another to save the best one. She worked tirelessly in the kitchen, cooking and baking and making preserves. She wore her white hair in a bun, with hundreds of pins. Occasionally a strand of hair would fall into her face and she'd brush it away with her forearm, because if her hands weren't in the washing-up suds, they'd be covered in pastry, or fruit or vegetable juice.

I started school again. I didn't make friends straight away. I was small for my age and very shy. I used to just go to school and come home, do my homework, and go back to school next day. I wasn't lonely.

Our school had a weekly motto. On Mondays the teacher would write it on the board for us to copy into our exercise books. They were things like: *'Deutsch sein heisst Charakter haben'* (to be German means to have character); or, *'Zäh wie Leder, flink wie die Windhunde und hart wie Kruppstahl soll ein Deutscher sein'* (a German should be tough as leather, quick as a greyhound, and hard as Krupp steel). This last motto led to a funny moment at a sports rally when the Burgermaster tried to use it in his speech, but got it wrong. 'Hard as Krupp steel, tough as a greyhound . . .' he said, but he couldn't finish with 'quick as leather' so he stumbled and went a bit red and petered out. My mother was highly amused and kept imitating him.

Another character-building motto was, 'I hope that I have proved myself worthy for a German soldier to give his life for me'. That motto disturbed me very much. I never felt valuable enough for anyone to sacrifice his life for me. It seems appalling to burden a child with such nonsense, but at the time I took it all in, and suffered.

There wasn't really enough room at Aunty Erna's, so my mum started to ask round for somewhere else, so as not to

Aunty Erna in Altenkirchen.

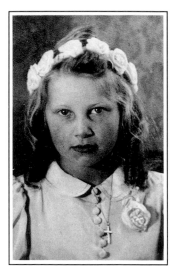

My friend Franziska, at her holy communion in 1942.

inconvenience Erna and her parents. She heard of a house with one spare room, and we went to look at it. As we turned in the gate I saw a girl in my class. I pointed her out to my mum. 'Don't you want to say hello to her?' She laughed.

I was always shy, and stared for a little while, not knowing how she'd react. But she came forward with her doll's pram.

'I'm Franziska, I'm in your class at school,' she said.

'I know,' I said, and told her that my name was Elsbeth and we might be living there. I pointed to the flat above, 18 Hochstrasse.

'I live at number 20,' said Franziska.

I ran back to my mother and told her. Then we went upstairs to talk to Frau Müller, who was a fat lady in her thirties. She seemed very friendly, and showed my mother the room, which had two beds and a cot, a wardrobe and a dressing table, two bedside cabinets and a stove. We would be sharing the bathroom, the WC and the kitchen with the family. My mum looked round and said we'd like to take it.

It was crowded in the Müller's house as well. At mealtimes we children often had to stand, because there weren't enough places at the table. Frau Müller had three children. The eldest was Helmuth, who was already a member of the Hitler Youth. Then came Hans-Gerd, who was in my class at school, and the youngest was Hertie, a girl the same age as Margret.

I enjoyed life in Altenkirchen. The war seemed a long way off, and Franziska became my best friend. I had meals round at her house, and shared her toys; mine had all been left behind in Düsseldorf, except for Grimm's *Fairy Tales* and a couple of other books. We used to play

Members of the Hitler Youth. After 1939 boys and girls had to join the Hitler Youth. Boys were taught a mixture of sport, war games and Nazi ideas.

school, using the door of the washhouse as the blackboard. We would write rows of sums on the board, and lists of new words to copy. We drew maps for geography lessons and these had to be copied into small exercise books we made. Whoever was teacher could mark them and enjoy putting red crosses next to wrong answers.

One of the nice things we did was to collect milk directly from a farmer. We got an aluminium milk-can from my uncle's shop and set off every morning to the nearby farm. Sometimes the farmer's wife had not milked the cows and we had to wait. She would take us into the cow-shed to watch her. The milk was so warm, steam rose up from the milking pail. When she'd milked the cows she poured the milk through a sieve to keep most of the cream to make butter. Then we watched her make the butter too, which was fascinating, and by the time we got home another lot of cream had formed. My mum would scoop it off and put it in the larder. At the weekend she would whip the cream, to go on the fruit flan she made, often with blueberries we picked in the woods. We enjoyed this

Mothers exchanging their children's shoes. Because of the shortages, when children had grown out of their shoes you could swap them for a bigger pair.

luxury through most of the war and felt lucky.

We were lucky where we lived too. There was woodland all round us, and right behind our flats was a sports ground. A little further on was a meadow where we played for hours, and picked dandelions for Franziska's rabbits. Through the meadow ran a little river, the Wied, which was lovely to bathe in in summer. Beyond this were woods full of blueberries. When the blueberry season was over, my mum took us on long walks to collect mushrooms and hazelnuts. The hazelnuts were for hazelnut cakes and biscuits, and for the chocolates she made for Christmas. She made them from cocoa and icing sugar and put them to dry on top of the wardrobe. Then she'd pack them away carefully. There was very little in the shops, and everything was rationed.

Germany was under blockade at this time, and things were scarce, so we often went out with the whole class to collect leaves and herbs for medicinal use. I enjoyed that a lot. No lessons, instead a nice stroll to the woods. We were usually given a particular kind of leaf or plant to collect and that way we learnt about botany.

Once we even picked nettles for the local hotel. They had found out that nettles can be cooked as spinach. I told my mum and we tried it too and we couldn't tell the difference when they were cooked, chopped and made up with a fine butter sauce and a little nutmeg. My mother and Erna were always inventing new recipes, or turning coats and altering dresses, unpicking old jumpers and knitting up new things for us with lovely patterns. Imagination wasn't rationed, and, for a while anyway, happiness wasn't either.

Near Leningrad

All the family had been getting letters from dad, but the post was slow, and took about ten days. He would tell us about the war, and wonder what might happen to him, and he would also talk about home, and think of the things he would do – like going bowling – when he got back. He wrote to Aunty Fränzi on 17 August, the very day we left for Altenkirchen: 'Received your letter last night and the card from the bowling club. Please give them all my regards ... I can hardly believe that Aunty Mariechen is going to get married again. It's very slow progress with us, every foot of ground needs to be fought for. I don't know whether we'll get more orders, or whether the war is over for us, but I think I'll be in Germany in 6–8 weeks' time.'

It must have been very worrying to get letters like the one that came three days later: 'Dear Fränzi, yesterday morning we lost another three men from our company. One of them died on his birthday yesterday, 19 August, and on the 18th he wrote in his diary: "Should I not be alive on my birthday, please greet my parents and brothers and sister." And in the early morning he was killed by a direct hit ... I had a piece of shrapnel go through my frying pan, two minutes later one flew above my head into a tree. You need to be lucky. But I think if something is going to happen one feels it beforehand. Well, dear Fränzi, that's all for now. Give my regards to all, also to your bowling friends. At Christmas you'll probably see me bowling a niner.'

To add to all this, when my dad heard we had left home, even though he was in the

Dad (on the far right) with some of the soldiers in his platoon.

middle of the fighting, he was very upset and cross: 'Dear Fränzi, I have now read the letter enclosed with your parcel of biscuits dated 17 August – I could only read it this morning, because it was dark last night. I could cry without stopping. You say Grete has left for the Westerwald. Her last letter was dated the 16 August and she asks me how I feel about her going to the Westerwald and now she's already there, one day later! I don't understand it. How can anyone leave their house and home and settle somewhere else? She's leaving everything behind just because there is a little bit of danger. When she was in Riesenburg she said that she wouldn't leave the house, and now she's left without my permission, even without writing beforehand.'

He was even worried about some money he sent: 'Dear Fränzi, I sent RM 200 to Grete on the 24th or 25th. Please see if you can get it at the Post Office and keep it for me. I had saved it and didn't buy myself a bottle of brandy, just because I wanted to cheer Grete up. I think I'll drop all my good intentions and be like I used to be. Then I'll have a wife who'll obey me.'

He was even complaining to his sister about mum: 'Grete wrote that she wanted a few weeks' peace. Not ten weeks ago she was with me in Riesenburg and had fourteen days of complete rest. She didn't have to do a thing. She had her meals served and the only thing she did for me was wash one shirt and one pair of pants the day before we moved out, and those I took with me in a wet state. I had washed my drill suit and everything else just to give her some peace. Does she think she can settle down somewhere with three children and do nothing? But I mustn't think about it anymore and get upset about it. I will come home sometime and then we'll do things the way we did them before the war...'

It was three weeks before my dad realized why we had left Düsseldorf and gone to Altenkirchen. Then he calmed down: 'Dear All, received a letter last night dated 24 August and now understand why Grete left so suddenly for the Westerwald. Now I am only anxious to find out what is damaged at home and what is left ... You can imagine how I'd love to come home, but there's no chance. Here it's slow progress. In the heavy rain our worst enemies are the roads through the forests. We are between Narwa and Novgorod [now called

Iwanskowskaja] and on the way south towards Nicolskoje. Our forces have encircled Leningrad and the day after tomorrow we shall probably force them to hand over the city. If not, it will be a hard nut to crack … Since the 25 August it's been bitterly cold here. Well otherwise not much to write. I am well and hope you are too. Has Fränzi got the RM 200? Grete will say what to do with it. Well, will close now and try and organize a few potatoes …'

All his letters now were from the fighting near Leningrad. This was written on 13 September: 'Dear Fränzi, I am still well and

The home-made Christmas card dad sent us from Russia in 1941. Father Christmas is saying 'It's a long way from home.'

healthy. We are a few kilometres from Leningrad and hope that when you receive this letter I will still be healthy and the city will be taken ... How are things with Aunty Mariechen? Is she married yet? How's everything at home? And how is the weather? From Monday afternoon the weather here was good, only the nights are cold and one has to take walks to keep warm, and since this morning it's been raining again. We could have done with a few more days clear weather for our aircraft. They could have supported us. I wish I knew how all this was going to end. I must close now. Hope you are all well. Greetings from your brother Heinz. PS Greetings to the bowling club.'

Though he must have been in the fighting nearly every day, my dad managed to write regularly to Elly and Fränzi and my mum. He told them more about the battle for Leningrad: 'From 9 to 12 September we attacked Leningrad and were 8 kilometres from the city. We are being relieved by the SS infantry who will take the town shortly. Well the SS can do anything, they are the only real troops fighting. We had heavy losses, because we had to take many bunkers and field positions. We all got "the death-sigh" here ... Most companies are still only 40 men strong despite relief, but they say we will get more troops and then we are supposed to storm towards Moscow. Others say we shall march to the Ukraine, or that we should be sent home, but I don't believe that. I am just anxious to find out what will happen.'

In the middle of all this he was still taking photographs: 'Dear Fränzi, the film you sent me is unfortunately no good for my camera because of the small feeder holes. If you get a film for me ask for a wooden spool not a metal spool...'

But the fighting never seemed to stop. This is from a letter of 25 November 1941: 'Dear Fränzi, best wishes from Russia from your brother Heinz. I thank God I am still alive and well, and hope you are too. Please forgive me not writing so much, but there's not much time. Every day we are in the fighting. Today was supposed to be a rest day but I think that we will attack. Since last night we have been under heavy Russian artillery fire ... You can imagine how we are all looking forward to a get-together back home, but who knows when that will be? ... It is difficult in attack, because in our division we have only about 20 operational tanks left out of 250 and they are *"weidwund wie der Jäger sagt"* – clapped out. But that won't deter us, the last battalion on the field will be a German one. They are also saying that there will be 18 new Panzer divisions, better than the ones we had before. Dear Fränzi, I will close now, a thousand greetings, your brother Heinz. PS Want to wish you a happy Christmas because this letter probably won't reach you any earlier. Heinz.'

Some letters must have made the family very sad. This was written the same day as the last one: 'Dear All, I want to send you a few lines. I am still well and hope you are too. Don't know what to write because we are at war and one day is much like the one before, always fighting and charging forward until we are victorious. Have written to Grete, Willy, and Fränzi, and got really homesick, because one mustn't think of home. Now I have to cry all the time and cannot stop, so, please leave me in peace for today. A thousand greetings, Heinz.'

Mid-winter 1941–2

This was a very difficult time for the soldiers in Russia because the deep snow and bitter cold made transport nearly impossible. Dad did not receive all the mail and parcels we sent and thought that we had forgotten about him.

The winter was not only cold in Russia. It was also one of the harshest winters in Germany, and I remember everything being covered in snow. In Altenkirchen we had to dress extra warmly and it was difficult to keep warm indoors with only one small stove and no coal to burn in it.

Christmas came and went and my mother was very agitated because she had not heard from dad for some time. The fate of our soldiers was on everybody's mind. The siege of Leningrad turned out to be the

Dad (on the right) in Russia, 1941.

doom of so many young men. The terrible cold immobilized vehicles and everything came to a standstill. War supplies, mail, ambulances with wounded on board, none of them could get through.

I still remember the day the postman came. He was usually a very jovial man, but he hesitated when he asked my mother for her signature for the registered letter he had. It was a blue envelope with official stamps on the back. My mother took the letter trembling. She opened it, read with an ashen face, threw the letter on the table, and left crying for our bedroom. My sister Margret and I stood bewildered and I began to tremble. Then Frau Müller picked up the letter. She looked shaken and reddened in the face from emotion. She read the letter. Then she said we'd better go and get Aunty Erna. Before that she showed it to me. I shook with every limb as I read

One of dad's photos taken in Russia in 1941, showing soldiers advancing through the snow towards a burning village.

that my father had been wounded in the right shoulder ... I didn't read any further. I could not bear it. I could not bear my daddy being hurt and being so far away from us. I burst into tears and followed my mother into our room. She lay on the bed, crying. My little sister Elfi was next to her, but didn't know what to do. She wasn't two yet. Margret still didn't realize what had happened.

Frau Müller came in with our coats. She dressed us up warmly and told us to show the letter to our relatives in the town. We both cried on the way. I'm sure Margret didn't know why, she just cried because we all cried. At the end of Hochstrasse a young Hitler Youth asked what was the trouble, why we were crying. 'My daddy is wounded,' I said and held out the letter. He read it and tried to console us, saying, 'Don't worry, being wounded means that he'll soon be home on leave. Don't cry any more.' With that he sent us on our way.

I am sure he'd read the entire letter, which went on to say how my father died a few days later. Obviously he didn't want to upset us any further. We walked solemnly through the small town to our aunt's house. We walked up the stairs, and in the door. I held the letter in my outstretched hand and sank to the ground near the door. I remained huddled up on the floor, joined by my sister, until Erna came towards us. She didn't say much at

When the German Army retreated from Moscow in 1942 they abandoned many of their guns and armed vehicles so they could get away as quickly as possible.

all, just patted our heads, got dressed and walked back with us to our mum and Elfi. I cannot remember what we did next, except some time later we were all dressed up again, my mum wearing her fur coat, on the way to the station.

In Düsseldorf three of my aunties were waiting, Aunty Fränzi, Aunty Hanni and Aunty Maria. They moved towards us in such an urgent way, clasping us to them and crying, 'You poor children!' It was terrible. We started crying again and I remember crying for a very long time, with one thing after another happening. It seemed endless, people coming and a mass being held, and everybody talking about my daddy and flowers arriving and condolence cards, and we had little letters with my dad's photograph in his uniform and the Iron Cross on top of his picture. He had been awarded the Iron Cross as well as the *Panzersturm Abzeichen* (Tank Charge Medal).

My father died twelve days after his 28th birthday. It was much later that I saw the letter again and learnt the circumstances of his death. He was wounded in the shoulder on 15 January, eight days after his birthday. Then, because of the impossible transport conditions, he had to be taken by dog sleigh, in the freezing cold, to an ambulance station. It took three days and three nights, and he was so exhausted and had lost so much blood that he died of heart failure the day after his arrival, on 19 January 1942.

A few weeks before I had made a Christmas card for my dad in school. We each had to make one and I sent mine to dad at the front. It is dated 11.12.41 and addressed to 'Sergeant Heinz Emmerich' (he had been promoted). It says: 'Dear

Daddy, many thousand Christmas greetings from your Elsbeth, Margret and Elfielein. I have made the card for you. It was the best in our class. We have been waiting a long time for your visit. When can you be with us again? Now I wish you all the best and an early holiday. Again, many greetings Elsbeth, Margret, Elfielein and Mutti.'

The card was returned to us. It was folded in the middle and the picture slightly rubbed away at the edge. My dad must have kept it in his wallet.

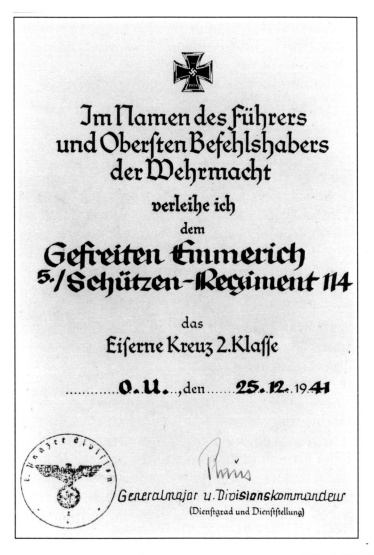

Im Namen des führers
und Obersten Befehlshabers
der Wehrmacht

verleihe ich

dem

Gefreiten Emmerich
5./ Schützen-Regiment 114

das

Eiserne Kreuz 2.Klasse

.............**O.U.**..,den.......**25.12.**19**41**

Generalmajor u. Divisionskommandeur
(Dienstgrad und Dienststellung)

This is dad's certificate, dated 25 December 1941, saying he had been awarded the Iron Cross.

CHAPTER 6
Moving to the Marktplatz

Altenkirchen was a small town, and soon people knew dad had died in the war. There was sympathy for mum, the young war widow, left with three lovely young daughters and living in just one room. Before long Aunty Erna brought a lady from the housing department to see us, Frau Schäfer, and with her help we moved a second time to a flat at the Marktplatz. The house was quite old with black beams. We had more space now, a bedroom, kitchen and living room, plus a small play room for us. My mother wrote to ask grandad to send some of her furniture, and the cupboard dad had made for Margret and me. When it arrived we found my grandad had packed our coffee-sets and the toys we had kept in the cupboard. Now we could ask other children to play with us.

When we moved to the Marktplatz I kept my friendship with Franziska, though now we had to walk a little distance to play with one another. One thing that did upset me was that Franziska didn't pass the exam to go to the High School the following year, so soon we wouldn't be at school together.

My mother had sent for her gas cooker, and she asked if gas could be put in the house. One day a young Polish prisoner of war came to dig a trench outside. At lunch-time mum went down to him and made signs for him to come up for something to eat. That was strictly against the rules. No mixing with the enemy or people from the workcamps! Mum didn't take much notice

This is the letter we sent to our friends and relatives announcing dad's death.

of such rules so he was soon sat at our dinner table. He didn't say a word. He seemed frightened and very hungry. We were also a bit frightened. What if he decided to attack us? Of course he didn't!

One day coming home from school I found my mother crying over a tub of washing. With a wooden stick she was stirring some sheets boiling on the stove. In her apron pocket she had a letter, and trying to explain she broke down again. Frau Müller took me aside and told me that my Aunty Elfriede had died after an operation in hospital. She was only twenty-six, and my mum's youngest sister.

She had two sons, Karlheinz and Horstdieter, and my grandmother immediately went off to look after them. With Anni, my mum's other sister, she took them to Breslau, in the far east of Germany. There they stayed, living with some relatives.

Mum's youngest sister, Elfriede, with Karlheinz, one of her sons.

A portrait of Hitler.
Every household was
meant to have one.

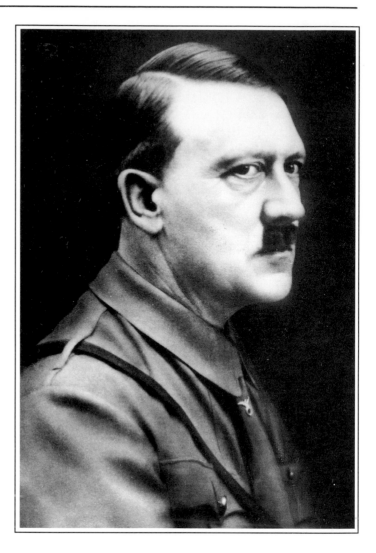

Another Christmas was coming. One day
there was a knock at the door and a woman
came in brandishing gifts. She had been
sent by the WHW (Winter Aid Work), who
usually collected warm clothing and
blankets for the soldiers at the front. But
this visit was for us, the children who had
lost their father fighting for the Führer.
She had a second-hand book with puzzles
and jokes and two small wooden dollies,
made by the HJ (Hitler Youth) and the
BDM (Federation of German Girls). We
thought the gifts were wonderful,
especially the dolls.

While the woman was talking in a sympathetic-sounding way to mum, her eye wandered around the room and suddenly she remarked that there was no picture of the Führer on the wall. My mother had to admit we didn't have one and I felt totally embarrassed, especially since she'd just brought us gifts and was so nice. So I went quietly to my school satchel and got out my reading book – I knew there was a full-page colour photograph of Adolf Hitler in the front. I tore out the page with the picture, took down an alpine landscape and put 'Mein Führer' in the frame over the landscape and hung it back on the wall. Then I gently pointed to the picture of Adolf Hitler and earned a huge smile from the woman with the gifts.

When the woman had gone my mother asked me, rather crossly, why I had done this and with those few words destroyed all the pride I had felt in coming to the rescue over the missing picture. Grown-ups are often difficult to understand!

My pride took another knock soon after when I came home from school and asked to send a parcel to a soldier at the front. Everybody was doing it, and I had heard on the radio that the soldiers especially liked getting parcels and letters from girls. I was a girl and I wanted to bring a little cheer to a soldier at the front. My mother and Aunty Erna just laughed. How humiliating! What was so ridiculous about that? Worse still, it seemed as if I should know why it was ridiculous!

Eventually, I insisted on knowing the answer. They said that soldiers appreciated parcels and letters from girls just a little bit older than myself. I was really hurt. Still, I kept on about it and mum got a small parcel ready which I

Members of the BDM
(Federation of German
Girls), giving the Nazi
salute.

addressed 'To an unknown soldier'. I was
overjoyed when some time later I received
a letter from a soldier who had received my
parcel.

In High School, I became a member of
the JM (Young Girls). We were all given
the entry forms in class to fill in there and
then, and told to take it home for our
parents' signature. Funnily enough, my
mother did not object to signing this, and
I enjoyed being in the JM. We had to attend
classes after school and learn about Adolf
Hitler and his achievements. We did
community work, singing to soldiers in
hospitals and making little presents for
them like bookmarks, or poems written out
neatly. We also went on hikes and collected
leaves and herbs for the war effort.

We even went away to camp. I thought
this might be exciting, but it wasn't like I
imagined, even though it was right in the
country in some lovely woodland. I was
shouted at within minutes of arriving, for

not picking up a bit of eggshell I'd dropped. Then there was reveille early in the morning, standing to attention in the freezing cold and singing whilst the flag was being hoisted. Then someone stole my purse. My 'holiday' was mainly doing what they told you to all the time, like standing to attention and raising our arms for the *Sieg Heil*.

I just longed to get home. Home! I longed to be back with mum and my sisters. I wondered if Margret would be back from her convalescent holiday in the Black Forest and if her rheumatism was better. I wanted to see everyone, and couldn't wait for the train to reach Altenkirchen. When we arrived we were all marched to the Marktplatz. Standing there watching people yelling commands, and listening to even more singing and shouts of *Sieg Heil*, I kept my eyes on the windows of our flat, wanting to see a face. Surely they'd look down, knowing I was home. But there was no one looking out for me!

When we were dismissed, I rushed to the house, ran upstairs and . . . the door was locked! I couldn't believe it! I picked up my bags and walked through the village to my Aunty Erna's. There she explained it all. Mum had gone to collect Margret from the Black Forest, and my grandparents would be coming the next day.

I went to meet my grandparents at the station, and it was marvellous to see them after such a long time. I had a lovely time with them, which made me nearly forget the terrible fortnight at the camp. Then my mother arrived a few days later with Margret and Elfi, Margret looking so brown and talking with a strange accent, after being away for eight months. At last we were together again, except for my dad.

Invitation to the Party

My mother spent a lot of time with us, going on long walks, collecting berries and nuts. She had friends round for meals occasionally and she read a lot of books. But she needed more to occupy her, and to help her stop thinking about my father, and before long she was doing athletics at the sports ground. We often went with her and had our own little 'Olympics' at the side of the track, while she was running or jumping or throwing the javelin. I was proud when she showed me her bronze medal, which was for doing well in many different sports, including swimming and running 2,000 metres through a forest.

She spent more and more time at her new hobby and soon obtained the silver medal. Then she was asked to coach young athletes. It involved a lot of travelling in the district, but she would take us along and we got to see several new places. We also went with her to training sessions on the field or in the sports hall, and were given a tennis ball or skipping ropes to play around with. Swimming was another of her interests and, as always, we all went along and had help learning to swim. All except me. It was somehow never my turn. I got quite annoyed about that.

I loved the water, and at least there was the river to splash about in. That was a bit further on from the swimming baths, in the small green valley called the Wiesental. The river was the Wied, which flows into the Rhine. We spent many long sunny afternoons there, in the shallow water near the bank.

I couldn't swim yet, and I remember one afternoon someone pulled my leg so I lost

Mum doing her sports exercises, in Altenkirchen. In the background is the house we lived in.

my balance, and I fell back so the water was over my face. I remember shouting 'Help!', but I couldn't get back properly on my feet because the current was pulling my legs from under me. I fell back again, trying to grab at the grass at the water's edge, but I was still being pulled along by the current and couldn't get a hold. I was panicking and thrashing out with my arms and in the distance I thought I heard someone shout my name, 'Elsbeth!' Then someone grabbed my arm above the elbow, so hard it hurt, and I came up again and there were two older boys holding on to me. They helped me out on to the bank. I coughed till it hurt and cried and cried, and while they were asking me if I was alright I ran away from them. I felt ashamed and embarrassed.

My mum hadn't even noticed any of this, I could see. There she was, enjoying the sun, smiling and chatting away nineteen to the dozen to her friend – completely unaware that I'd just nearly drowned. She hardly even looked up when I went up to her still crying and spluttering. When I told her I very nearly drowned, all she did was laugh and say, oh dear but you didn't drown darling and now you're alright, aren't you? I couldn't believe it. I was suddenly so mad at mum it almost made me feel better straight away. Perhaps that was the idea.

My mother was becoming a sports personality. Even my teacher stopped in the street to talk to her about some sports event. Her new hobby appeared to agree with her. She totally immersed herself in it and seemed quite happy. But whenever you are feeling too happy something happens to spoil it.

This time it was another knock at the door and enter a stranger. A strange man with notebook and pencil and a Nazi pin in his lapel. He said that he'd heard about my mother and her achievements. He had assumed that she was a member of the Party and only found out that she was not when he checked his records. (Of course anyone who referred to the 'Party' meant the Nazi Party. There was only one.)

No doubt that was just an oversight, he went on, and she would join? He had his pencil at the ready but my mother froze over and said firmly 'NO'. She did not want to become a member of the Party. He wanted to know her reasons and she said that she had reasons of her own. He didn't understand. 'You realize you cannot keep

The certificate of mum's Silver Sports Medal.

your position as coach to our young girls, unless you are a member of the Party?' My mum said surely coaching had nothing to do with politics, and that being a Party member would not make her a better coach. However, the man with the Party pin in his lapel knew better and my mother had to give up a much cherished job.

I remember some of the conversations mum had with various people after this. She learned that people who refused to become members of the Party simply lost their jobs. If you had a shop, for instance, you either became a Party member or closed down. All shopkeepers had to display a little sign in the window showing that they were a Party member: 'NSDAP' – 'National Socialist German Workers' Party.'

CHAPTER 7
To the Shelters

For some time after people had started talking about the war I didn't really know what it meant. Now I was getting an idea. War meant being bombed, losing good friends and neighbours, and, most of all, it meant losing a much loved father. I could not really get over this. All my prayers were in vain. I felt let down. I was angry with God, but then I didn't dare to be too angry, because I was still praying that it was all a mistake and my daddy would come home one day. My prayers affected my dreams. Many times I woke up thinking dad had returned from the battlefield to be with us once again.

The war entered the games we played. In one game we drew a circle on the ground and divided it up into countries. We had to throw a stone into the right space and if we missed we had to forfeit some land. Obviously, Hitler's ambition to get more territory for Germany – *Lebensraum* – was the idea for this game.

The other war-time game was collecting shrapnel and mementoes from crashed planes or bombs. We had not suffered from bombings in Altenkirchen so far, but a few planes had crashed in the area. We often watched the fighter planes, flying so low we could see the pilots in their cockpits. It was terrifying!

I remember the day when I saw an American pilot being led through the town handcuffed. I was in the school playground and could not keep my eyes off him. He was dressed in a very pale blue flying suit. I had never seen such clothing before. The pilot was a young man and he looked sad, his head hanging down so he seemed to stare at his hands. His step was slow and sluggish. My heart sank. This poor fellow. He was far away from home, so far away! As far as my dad had been!

He was guarded by two men with rifles. I thought no one should ever treat another person like that. I wondered what would happen to him and felt afraid for him.

An American Flying Fortress making a daylight raid over Berlin. Sometimes fighter planes flew so low we could see the pilots.

Meanwhile, Hans-Gerd showed me pictures about the war. Pictures of Japanese weapons and knives, pictures of torture which our enemies would use against us, if we were caught or if we lost the war. I was petrified! There were cages, the insides full of metal spikes, so when the door was shut, the spikes would go straight through the victim. These were drawn on the leaflets scattered by aeroplanes.

I don't know how he got hold of these because I didn't see any of them come down. But they did make me very frightened and I decided that if the enemy should come and conquer us, I would try and talk to them to save my mother and sisters. I would tell them that we had already lost our daddy and that we would not do anything against them. In my

Many people spent night after night in air raid shelters like this one.

imagination I could see myself handcuffed, facing a lot of armed men and pleading for our lives. I was even prepared to give my life if my mother and sisters would be spared. I knew I wouldn't be able to watch the death of any one of my family.

Thoughts like these would make me so frightened, I thought my heart would stop. I often cried out at night and my mother had to come to my bed and comfort me. I remember once saying, 'I think my heart is going to stop, Mummy!' My mother felt my heartbeat and reassured me that all was well. She wiped my tears and told me to go back to sleep.

The war was also coming to Altenkirchen in another way. Up until now we had little bother from bombs. But now we spent a great deal of time in air raid shelters. We went to one of the bigger shelters. This was the town prison, which was at one corner of the square where my school was. It was a very dark building which had cellars with arched ceilings and a floor of earth. There were wide backless benches for two rows of people and nothing else. It was bleak and frightening, but my mum said the arched ceilings would stand up to bombing much better than flat ceilings.

We spent days and nights in the cellars of the prison. We were usually on the last bench in the third room. We got to know the people who went to the same place each time. We learnt to pass the time talking, reading, solving puzzles, making small things out of paper. Most women used to knit, including my mother, who became quite skilled at this new form of entertainment.

When the all-clear went, we would go home and cook a quick meal. Often my mum would leave some potato or vegetable soup on the small stove, so that when we came out, there was something warm to eat.

Because air raid alarms were frequent, the baker had to produce his bread whenever he could, and we got used to dashing round to his bakery for hot bread. As we ran home, carrying the bread in our aprons to save us getting burnt, it was lovely picking at the hot crusty loaves.

Once or twice we used another shelter, which was highly recommended for its safety. It was an old mine. To get there we had to cross the Wiesental and then the bridge, and even when we got to the mineshaft I was terrified of going in. I trembled every moment we were inside. There were benches on either side of the mine, but a constant drip from above left a pool of water that seeped up through the wooden slats under our feet.

One day we were running across the meadow to get to the mine when out of nowhere we saw two planes coming in low over the tree-tops. My mum, who was ahead of Margret and myself, carrying Elfi, screamed, 'Get down! get down! quick! down!' As we threw ourselves to the ground I saw bombs falling from the planes, immediately overhead. I froze, my face buried in the grass. But in a second or two there were explosions from further on ahead of us. We were safe! The bombs had travelled in the direction of the planes' flight and fallen not vertically but at an angle, exploding behind the mountain.

We picked ourselves up and ran on to the mine. I was trembling with shock. Later we decided it was too risky crossing the open meadow after an air raid warning, and never used the mine shelter again. One experience like that was enough.

Retreat

At first it was just a trickle, but soon there was a steady flow of German soldiers, retreating from the front. Altenkirchen was a meeting point for all routes, and the troops would stop to rest in the Marktplatz.

One day my mother was looking out of the window as yet another group halted outside our house.

'It's the *Hohenstauffen*,' she said. 'That is Hermann's regiment.' Hermann was the son of Frau Schmid, the very good landlady in Riesenburg, near Königsberg, where my mother had stayed when visiting my father. He had, like his mother, kept in touch and written to mum frequently. However, she had not heard from him for a while. He had been drafted into the SS when he left High School. My mother went outside to ask if they knew Hermann.

German prisoners being escorted across the bridge at Remagen. We knew the Americans were getting closer.

Hermann had already made his own enquiries. He realized that Altenkirchen was where mum lived and could hardly believe his luck when his regiment stopped at the Marktplatz. Before my mother returned, Hermann was knocking on our door. He was very young, just eighteen years old, but he was very battle-weary. He was slow and sad and seemed to be carrying the grief of the world. We did not have a bathroom in this old house, but it was marvellous for him to be in a house, with a family he knew, and able to wash and shave in privacy. He ate at our table and afterwards he told us some of the things he had suffered.

He'd been an ambulance driver in a convoy of three, carrying badly wounded men. Being in a Red Cross vehicle did not save him from attack, because Red Cross vehicles had been used for military purposes. The two other ambulances had been hit in air attacks, and with one driver killed and one wounded, Hermann had to deal with the wounded on his own. A week later he had to repair his own vehicle when that was hit. He said more and more wounded were dying because of the shortage of ambulances. This would have upset me a great deal if I'd known then what I found out much later. I only knew after the war that my father died because they couldn't get him to hospital quickly enough.

Hermann soon left with his regiment and it was the last we heard or saw of him. At the time we thought that he must have been shot by the Allied Forces, since there was a rumour that SS men were shot on sight. Aunty Fränzi, Aunty Greti and Uncle Walter said they witnessed the shooting of a very young SS man in April 1945, on

about the 17th or 18th. He was shot by Americans, they said, in a brickyard opposite their house. They went to him afterwards to try to find out who he was, and inform his family, but his identification papers had gone, as well as his jacket and boots.

The rest of Hermann's family were never heard of, and since they had always kept in touch, we think that they must have gone down in one of the ships from East Prussia to Scandinavia. Several had sunk in rough weather.

After that soldiers were everywhere,

Six B-24s making a bombing raid in northern Germany. Daylight raids became a frequent terror for us in Altenkirchen.

even in our air raid shelters. From their talk my mother gathered that the war would soon end. The artillery could be heard every night and it seemed that little bit closer each time. Once again I was very frightened. What would happen to us? Would we be blown up? Would we survive the artillery then face the enemy? Would we be tortured, killed? I kept thinking of my daddy and how he had to face up to death all alone in Russia. Could I be brave? I didn't think so. I was very frightened.

I wasn't the only one though. Even some of the soldiers were afraid. They said, 'If we're caught wearing a uniform, we're done for. And if we're caught not wearing a uniform, we're still done for – if one of those fanatical German officers finds us.' They must have meant that they would be shot as deserters – soldiers running away.

Many ordinary people were afraid too. They would have loved to hang out a white flag, but they were petrified of German officers, still trying to 'defend every foot of soil'. They would shoot the men of any household that hung out a white flag.

That was not all. Almost daily *'Jabos'* (*Jagdbombers* or Spitfires) appeared in the sky. They came howling down and shot at anything that moved. Our house had several holes from machine-gun fire. One went right through the toilet, which fortunately wasn't occupied at the time. Once they appeared so suddenly that we didn't have time to run to the shelter, but made a hasty escape to our own cellar, where we stood trembling, my mother holding us three in her arms.

'If only daddy was here,' I cried.

'He wouldn't be able to help us either,' said my mum, and I realized that she was right. I just wanted us to be together.

Devastation

The war was coming closer. We could hear explosions as retreating German soldiers blew up bridges to prevent the Americans from following them. We heard the bridge at Remagen blown up. We were quite close to Remagen and there was a lot of fighting going on there. The German soldiers even dynamited tiny river crossings – wooden bridges spanning streams almost narrow enough to jump across.

We'd had quite a peaceful and even enjoyable time in Altenkirchen, but now the war was raging here too with daily air raid warnings, low-flying aircraft attacks, explosions, and artillery fire thumping away in the background. For a while we hardly seemed to emerge from the shelters.

On one particular day we were running to the shelter after the air raid warning. We could already hear the bombers. Margret used to scream when she heard the sirens or the low-flying aircraft, and she was always first in the shelter. Now she was hysterical again and ran straight into the first shelter, the one on the corner, which was the restaurant shelter. I stood outside with Elfi and told mum that Margret had gone in. She ran down to fetch her. She brought her out and we ran on to our usual prison shelter.

I remember we didn't get to our usual place in the third room, but stayed in the first one because my mother had met one of the soldiers she'd been talking to the day before. Margret and I picked our way round towards the third room, to be with our usual group and meet some of our friends. But before we reached them the most horrifying explosions and vibrations shook

Nuremburg was badly bombed. These people are picking their way through the ruined streets.

us and the earth seemed to sway. Margret screamed and ran to my mother and clung around her neck. I followed her, quietly but stiff with fear. Mum held the three of us tightly in her arms. Margret started praying aloud non-stop. The explosions went on and on. There were whistling noises followed by a chain of explosions close together: thump, thump, thump, thump. On and on it went, on and on.

Then it stopped. It was over, and we were alive! We were still looking around at each others' faces, in the sudden stillness, when the trap door was thrown open and a woman with blood on her face and dress burst in. She waved her arms hysterically screaming: 'They're all dead, they're all dead!' Aghast, some of the people in the shelter pushed outside.

I waited, watching and listening. A rabbit came hopping into the shelter.

Eventually I dared to follow. I could hardly believe what my eyes told me. Everything had changed! Where one street of houses had stood, there were heaps of bricks and rubble. On the other side there were parts of houses standing, with the indoors showing, upstairs bedrooms with wallpaper and fireplaces and curtains swinging in the smoke. The school-yard where we'd played the day before was a line of craters. There were fires and mountains of rubble where there had been a main road, and there was a stench from explosives and burning.

And it was still. Not a soul could be seen apart from the small crowd round us that had emerged from this prison cellar.

Then mum, carrying Elfi, and Margret, the soldier and I tried to make our way to our house. We had to clamber across rubble and jump over fires. The soldier carried us

through one burning area. The road had gone. Everything had changed beyond recognition.

Eventually we reached our house. It was still standing, though badly damaged. A man was trying to dislodge a burning mattress from the roof. The front door had blown away. Through the rubble we clambered upstairs, saw the devastation in our rooms and decided to leave. It was uninhabitable.

We went to Aunty Erna's house. Amazingly, that was standing, though everything around it, including Aunty Erna's friend's jewellery shop, was flattened. Erna was there, and she threw her arms round us. We were all just glad to be alive. Then we went back to our house for some food and a change of clothes. We put them on over the clothes we were already wearing. Margret and I each grabbed our favourite doll and stood

Soup kitchens were set up to help people who had lost their homes through bomb damage.

Young Nazis captured in Nuremburg. By the end of the war, very young men were being called up to fight.

outside the house clutching them. But mum said we couldn't take them. 'We'll come back for them one day. Just for now, we'll hide them,' she said, and we went into our cellar and hid our dolls in a pile of potatoes. No one could find them, mum said, they'd be quite safe.

We heard that all the people in the restaurant shelter had died, all the people in the justice building, and all the people in the old school shelter. Only the old prison had stood up to the bombings, as mum had said it would. If we had followed my sister into the restaurant, we would have all died.

We heard horrendous stories of people being buried alive. There was a car firm where rescuers couldn't reach trapped people whom they could hear calling and knocking. My aunty's friends were never found. Their jeweller's shop was wiped out completely. My aunty and some other friends dug for weeks but only found a three inch square of a dressing gown.

We learned later that the small town had taken seventeen waves of bombing that day, and two-thirds of the population had died. The Burgermaster, who was also the headmaster of my old school, had been asked by the Americans to hand the town over, but he was a fanatical Nazi, and wouldn't give in. In his shiny boots and brown uniform, he was going to fight for every foot of German soil.

Of course he didn't do any fighting. There wasn't any fighting. There was only the bombing, which killed two-thirds of all the people in Altenkirchen. They died because he went brainlessly on being a fanatical Nazi.

Perhaps he realized. He was found later in the woods. He'd hanged himself.

CHAPTER 8
Leaving Altenkirchen

The village where my grandad was born, Burbach, was only 30 kilometres from Altenkirchen. Mum decided we should go there.

It might have been a pleasant walk through the countryside if it had not been for low-flying aircraft, shooting at everything that moved. Every time we heard them approaching, we had to dive into the ditches dug by German soldiers. I hated getting muddy all over. Even my best coat was covered in mud and so was my school satchel, which was stuffed with underwear and socks.

A German despatch-rider passed us. A little later we saw his motor bike in the ditch. He had been shot dead by the Spitfires.

Elfi was still not five, but she stood up to the trek like the rest of us. Aunty Erna came with us, perhaps to show us the way or to make sure we got there alright. I know she went back to Altenkirchen later on, to be with her parents. I remember them both, my mother and Aunty Erna, urging us on. 'Not much further to go,' they'd say, and on we went.

Eventually we reached Burbach. The first house in the village belonged to my grandad's family. I remember it had an enormous dung heap right outside. Even indoors the sickly manurey smell seemed to hang in the air; it was not to my liking. We were hugged and cuddled by Aunty Paula, one of mum's cousins. She said we were to stay at a farm owned by one of my grandad's friends.

We had to sleep in his loft, where he stored apples. It was quite an experience, climbing up a ladder to bed every night, and sleeping under the rafters on prickly hay. We had blankets and pillows as well. Still, not a bomb had fallen on Burbach and that reassured us. But we could see bombing raids on other places not far away, and even Altenkirchen was bombed again, for some unknown reason. No one was trying to hold or defend it any more. All the soldiers wanted was to go back home. We kept seeing them making their way on their own or in twos and threes, trying to avoid being caught by the Americans or the German troops still fighting.

We hadn't been at the farm long when Aunty Anna, another of mum's cousins, invited us to stay with her. She was the local midwife and had two sons, Hermann

Women taking a coffin through the streets of Berlin. It was horrible to see the makeshift coffins in Altenkirchen.

and Werner. She had the most modern house in Burbach, the last one in the village, at the top of the hill. Aunty Anna had other people in the house as well, a family from Troisdorf, with three children.

Aunty Paula made bread for all of us. But my mum, the woman from Troisdorf and Aunty Anna had to go to a mill in another village for flour. This was usually a day-long trip and sometimes my mother would take Elfi with her. Aunty Paula also made butter in her farmhouse, each portion in a lovely egg shape. I'd go to Burbach any day for some of that bread and that butter!

Then my aunt's house was needed by some retreating Austrian troops, so we had to give up our beds and sleep on the floor. The Austrians used to celebrate something every night and left lots of empty bottles about, which we used to drain the last drops out of. We loved getting slightly tipsy on the remains of the Austrians' parties.

I can't remember the reason, but one day we had to go back to Altenkirchen. Perhaps it was just to get some money out of the post office. The soldiers, this time some Germans who had also been staying at my aunt's house, gave us a lift on the back of their lorry. When we arrived, we were shocked. Altenkirchen seemed even worse than when we left. Apart from the devastation, there were rough coffins piled at the side of the road, and the stench from all the bodies hung over the town and made me feel sick. The coffins were hastily hammered together; there was no time even to plane the wood. They were made from rough planks with the bark still on the sides, and the boards did not fit properly against one another, so I could see parts of the bodies through the gaps and slits. It was terrible.

I didn't go to Altenkirchen again at that time, but mum wanted to keep an eye on the house in the Marktplatz and on our belongings and she made one or two more trips. It was after one of these that she told me my doll Marie-Lotte had been stolen. Our milkwoman had seen a Polish woman leave our house with the beautiful doll under her arm. She must have been taking the potatoes and found the doll. My mum said that the Polish child would be happy having such a beautiful doll, but in my heart I cried for Marie-Lotte. I missed her and wanted her.

On another occasion Herr Schmoll, a pilot, who had been in Africa, took mum to Altenkirchen on an army lorry. She went to get her record player and radio. Soon we were hearing some of the old songs again, like Zarah Leander's 'I know that one day a miracle will happen', or some of mum's favourite operetta songs from *The Land of Smiles*, *The Merry Widow* and *Masked Ball*. We also had a record entitled *'Freunde, das Leben ist lebenswert!'*, or, 'Friends, life is worth living!'

Yes, that was one of the songs we used to play in the midst of everything: 'Friends, life is worth living!'

Americans!

One morning the German soldiers had disappeared. Everyone had gone, vanishing into thin air without a word.

The day before we had seen American tanks and jeeps along the horizon, but we were almost used to them being near. It was just that no one could imagine what it would be like once they actually came. My mother seemed to be the only person who wasn't getting into a panic. The most worried were the men, who were afraid of being shot. I could tell how afraid they were and their fear transferred to me. I just could not work out what would happen to us. Would we be shot, or tortured? Would we even survive the artillery? Whenever I thought about all these things I grew taut with fear.

In the meantime, we still needed to live, and eat. Flour was required for the baking. Just once, earlier on, I'd gone with mum, Aunty Anna and the young woman from Troisdorf on their trip to the village next to Burbach. In the depth of the forest we came upon enormous stocks of ammunition left behind by the fleeing troops. I remember walking through this maze of piled cases and boxes, feeling terrified that a plane might shoot into it and set it all off. Nothing would have been left of us, if those piles of shells and bullets had gone up.

Though the Americans were getting nearer, my mother and the rest of the women were resolute. They were determined to get flour for the bread, because without bread we'd starve. They were prepared to take their chances, and there was no question now of any of us children going with them just for the pleasant walk.

On this particular day we were playing quite happily together, when we heard shooting quite close. We stopped dead in our play, and listened. The sound of shooting came slowly nearer, then we heard the sound of gears changing and engines revving, from vehicles approaching through the woods. This was it! The Americans were coming! We still couldn't see anything, and we were all so

In June 1944 Allied troops landed on the Normandy coast, and by August were marching through Paris.

frightened that we didn't have time to talk much or discuss what to do. We headed for the back door which led to the wash-kitchen.

We looked around wildly for somewhere to hide. Werner ran across to the huge wash-tub, pulled himself up and with a wave of his legs, vanished into it. We followed him in, and all seven of us, like the seven little goats in the story, hid in the big wash-tub! Werner pulled the lid over our heads, leaving it a bit open, so that we could see the road and what was going on. The road bent around my aunty's house, so we had a perfect view along it.

After a minute or two of silence and heavy breathing, we saw them! Americans in their jeeps, shooting! But what was that? Their rifles were pointed towards the sky. They weren't shooting at anybody. They were just shooting in the air!

That was a relief! But we still preferred to stay in our hiding place for a while until it became too uncomfortable. After a few minutes everything was quiet, so we all

American soldiers talking to a German family. We were amazed to find that the Americans were not the monsters we had been told they were.

crept out. The Americans had gone again. A convoy had driven through the village and gone on. We couldn't wait for our mothers to get back home to tell them.

We were all frantic with excitement when they returned. My mother already knew that the Americans had come. She just stayed as calm as ever and told us not to worry. Then, while we were all in the kitchen, the door bell went. My aunty answered the door. Outside stood the most gigantic American one could imagine. He must have been well over six foot and his uniform made him look twice as big. He had a round of ammunition around his waist and a Tigerhead on his breast pocket. Immediately, my heart trembled again and I tried to be invisible.

'Does anyone speak English?' he asked.

The woman from Troisdorf went forward and said, 'Just a little'.

I had started to learn English in school and thought, I could have said that. But I was too afraid.

I was still only shallow breathing, uncertain if they would not suddenly decide to do something to us. After all, we had been told so many things about the enemy, and now they were here; who knew what might happen.

The American called one of the other soldiers and they both went through the house, looking at every room. When he finished his inspection, we were informed, with the woman from Troisdorf interpreting, that the house was needed by the American forces. We were told what we could take along and what we had to leave behind. My mother's radio and record player were two of the things we had to leave behind.

My aunty went to stay with Aunty Paula

at the bottom of the village, while we went back to grandad's friend, where we had slept before in the loft. I don't know where the family from Troisdorf went. They may even have decided to return to Troisdorf.

That same evening, we were already in bed in our hayloft when we saw a group of Americans just outside the farmhouse. They were trying to talk to some young girls. They gave them cigarettes and chewing gum. We were amazed!

The next morning, we were sitting at the breakfast table when some Americans came into the farmhouse. They gave us tinned powdered egg, and oats. I couldn't believe it. They were giving us food! And to top it all, they handed out chewing gum! We had never had chewing gum in our lives. Soon there were boys and girls in the village following the Americans around calling out, 'Cigarettes, please!' Or 'Chewing gum, please!' They seemed to like being followed. They sat in their jeeps throwing out chewing gum and cigarettes. For the first time in my life I saw black people. They too were huge!

During the next few days every so often we heard shots. 'Oh, that will be an SS man,' the people in the village said. Later we found out that the Americans had tried shooting at fish in the river.

I became so happy and totally relieved and exhilarated when I realized that the Americans were not 'the enemy' as I had been taught, but normal human beings, friendly and generous. No one was being shot and no one was being tortured. I didn't have to plead for my mother or my sisters' lives.

I cannot remember ever feeling happier or more relieved than I did after the Americans came to our little village.

CHAPTER 9
Back to Altenkirchen

It was time to go back to Altenkirchen. The town was a tragic place. There were heaps of rubble everywhere and rows and rows of coffins. People were walking along the rows, bending over coffins, looking in to see if they could recognize their relatives. The stench of bodies still hung over everything.

On a large hoarding put up where a hotel had stood, I saw a poster of Hitler with blood dripping from his mouth and his hands. He was drawn like a cannibal. I didn't understand. Throughout the war I had not heard a single bad word said against him and suddenly here he was portrayed as a monster thirsty for blood.

People I had known throughout the war, people who had run off eagerly in their brown uniforms to the Nazi rallies, suddenly hated Hitler. People like the man in the flat above us. We'd often passed him on the stairs in his fine SA gear. Now he was saying how awful Hitler was. At the age of eleven, such people gave me my first real lesson in human nature. I never again believed something just because someone told me so. I realized I had to make up my own mind about what I thought. I had to be in charge of my own life, and decide what was right and wrong.

My mother had taken some of our things to Aunty Erna and some to a friend of hers. When we returned we found that nothing had been destroyed by bombs, but a lot of things had been stolen or soiled. My father's camera and binoculars had gone. All his suits had been taken. We found the bottoms of one pair of trousers that had

This cartoon from a Russian poster shows Hitler as a cannibal. He is eating the countries of Europe. During the war nothing bad was ever said about Hitler. Seeing pictures like this at the end of the war was confusing.

been cut off to make them fit. Mum even saw someone walking round the town in a suit that she recognized.

She was, as always, quite philosophical about this. 'They need clothes,' she said. But I knew it hurt her to think of my dad's tailor-made suits, and his other clothes, being worn by strangers.

What hadn't been stolen had been deliberately soiled. Jars of jam and preserved fruit had been poured over table and bed linen and clothing, which was all mouldy and stank. There was no bed linen or clothing in the shops, so we couldn't replace them. Instead, we just washed and washed them, then took them to the riverbank and spread the sheets and pillow cases on the grass in the meadow. There we kept pouring water from the river over them. It was our job to sprinkle the sheets with a watering can. Slowly, very slowly, they became cleaner. It took ages.

There was no water coming out of the taps, so we also had the job of queuing up for drinking water. We would stand for ages with a couple of jugs in a long line of people waiting to collect water that ran slowly from a spring. But we soon grew used to it. The water queue was a place where we learned about other people's war experiences, and of course we ended up telling our own stories.

Women forming a chain to clear rubble from a bombed-out building.

This was when we heard stories of violence after the fighting ended. We were told of women who had been killed for the fur trimmings on their coats. In their fear, people would put heavy boards behind their doors at night, especially if the house had been damaged.

Our house in the Marktplatz was too badly damaged to live in. We were allowed to stay in the Schäfers' house for a while, because they were still away somewhere. That house was damaged too and the windows were roughly boarded up. Children make the best of things though, and we used to enjoy being able to go in and out through a hole in the wall.

One morning Margret and I made a worrying discovery – a drawer full of Nazi flags. In our bedroom! Herr Schäfer was Regional Sports Warden and had all kinds of flags in this drawer, every one with a swastika in its design. We were terrified, and didn't know what to do. What if the Americans found them? They would think they were ours and take revenge! It was already forbidden to display a swastika in any form. My mother had even filed the swastika off her sports medals.

After a frantic discussion, we decided to hide the flags under the mattress, and sleep on them. The Americans would never find them there! I started lifting them out of the drawer while Margret held the mattress up for me to push them under. Suddenly we heard voices outside in the street. Foreign voices! We tiptoed to the window and peeped down. There, right below us so we could see the tops of their heads, were three American soldiers. We were terrified again. Had they come to the house to look for Nazi flags, like the 'nice' man long ago, but the other way round?

No, they hadn't, we realized a minute later. We heaved huge sighs of relief, as we watched them stroll down the road with a couple of girls.

Starting Again

Meanwhile, families tried to get together and find out who was still alive and who was not. There were so many of us!

First my grandfather came all the way from Düsseldorf on a bicycle without tyres. He was a very restrained man, but he cried for joy when he saw us and could hold us in his arms. He stayed with us for a few days whilst mum was busy making arrangements to leave Altenkirchen and return to Düsseldorf. Then Aunty Fränzi came as well, also on a bicycle (with tyres), to see if we were still alive.

Mum somehow organized a lorry to take us and our belongings to Düsseldorf. We children had to sit in the back of the lorry amongst our furniture. It was a long slow bumpy journey.

Our house, our new house of not so long ago, was almost falling apart. There were cracks in the sides. Some of it just wasn't there. Uncle Walter, who had a demolition and construction business, came with his crew and they put an iron brace into the walls to pull the sides together. They made it safe enough to live in, but it still looked as if a bomb had hit it – which of course it had!

But it was a hopeful time, too. In the garden we were thrilled to find ripe mirabelles on the ground. There were some plums on the small golden plum tree grandad had planted. In the back he'd

At the end of the war we could start to rebuild our family life. Here we are in Düsseldorf. From left to right, Elfi, Aunty Fränzi, my cousin Heinz, Aunty Maria, my cousin Viktor, me, Mum, Margret.

grown some tobacco. It became our job to cut the huge leaves into fine shreds, roll them up and make them into cigarettes for my grandad.

Then I remember the day we received a letter from Halle. It was a registered letter from grandma. She wrote to say she was well and so was Aunty Anni, and the boys were fine after walking all the way from Breslau. She now wanted grandad to meet her in Halle.

It was another joyous reunion. Grandad returned with grandma and the boys, Aunty Anni and her husband, Uncle Richard. The much damaged house had to serve as living quarters for all and we used to sleep two to a bed. Next my Uncle Karl arrived, wondering how his boys had fared during the war, and for a while he also stayed with us.

Despite the hardship, they were good days. We were rebuilding our family life and happy to find that we had not lost anyone else. We were coming together again.

But it was hard. There was very little of anything in the shops, and most items of food were really scarce. We had to find ways of managing. Aunty Maria and Uncle Victor had a bakery and my mother started working for them, so at least our daily bread was secure. Uncle Willy was still working in the abattoir, so occasionally there was a bit of bacon. Another uncle could get cooking oil. One thing we couldn't get, not in the town, was potatoes. My grandmother had to brave the train and return to the countryside. There were very few trains, and people were crammed into them like cattle, but in the country she could exchange some of our bits of jewellery or fur for a sack of potatoes. She said you had to sit on your potatoes on the way home or they'd be stolen.

Once mum sent me on a bus driven by a neighbour, Herr Materne, all the way to Altenkirchen. I was carrying a bag of sugar which I had to trade for a sack of potatoes. Herr Materne looked after me during the journey there and back, and delivered me and the potatoes safely into the hands of my mother.

I even began school again. I hadn't been inside a school for a year and a half, but now my mother took me to the Luisenschule, a grammar school for girls. I had to attend for the rest of the year and then stay in the Sexta class again because I didn't know enough English to move into the Quinta.

I may have missed out on my English lessons, but I had learnt something far

In Düsseldorf 93 per cent of the houses were destroyed. This woman is trying to do some washing in her half-demolished house.

more important. I had learnt not to believe everything people said. I had realized that other nations are made up of people just like ourselves, and that to call other people 'the enemy' is a tactic used by the people who make propaganda.

I had always believed that what adults told you was the truth. I'd believed that my dad was stronger than everything. Now I had learned differently.

This was the time when I began to think back over what had happened. It dawned on me how often my grandfather had been taken away by strange men in overcoats, and I asked mum more and more questions.

To many of the questions there were answers, but I am still at a loss to understand what power held our country in such a frightening grip. I still don't know why my father had to die at the age of twenty-eight with no loved one near him.

Important Dates

1933   *January* Hitler becomes Chancellor of Germany.

1939   *1 September* German troops invade Poland. The Polish war lasts only three weeks.
3 September Britain and France declare war on Germany.

1940   *May* The German Army invades France, going direct for Paris instead of along the coast, which was what the generals advised. Paris is captured, and France defeated.

1941   *22 June* German troops cross the Russian border. Hitler thinks Russia will collapse within a month. No detailed plans are made.
July Russian troops are defeated in great numbers but, to the amazement of the German generals, the Russian Army does not collapse. Hitler changes his plan to send his armies straight for Moscow, and instead orders them to capture Leningrad.
30 August Leningrad is surrounded. The siege begins. It was to last for nearly three years ('900 days').
October Snowstorms, rain and mud. A terrible winter was beginning.
2 December The German troops are halted 25 km outside Moscow. The Russians now launch a counter-attack.

1942   *23 August* The German Sixth Army begin the battle for Stalingrad. After three months of hard fighting they take control of the city.
18 November In a massive counter-attack, the Russians surround Stalingrad, trapping 300,000 German troops.

1943   *February* The German Army at Stalingrad surrenders. The Russian armies start their push towards Germany.

1944   *6 June* D-Day. The Allies land on the coast of Normandy, in France, which is still occupied by Germany. From there they start to advance across France.
20 July A bomb meant to kill Hitler explodes at a meeting of Hitler and his generals.
15 August The Allies land in the south of France.
19 August Paris is freed.

1945   *7 March* American troops cross the Rhine.
30 April Russians capture Berlin. Hitler commits suicide.
8 May Germany surrenders.